Wash, scrub, brush!

a book about keeping clean

Mick Manning and Brita Granström

W

FRANKLIN WATTS
LONDON•SYDNEY

Someone's having a party –
and we're all going.
But first we must be clean and tidy.
We need to…

wash, scrub, brush!

Animals, birds – even insects
wash, scrub and brush!

There are more harmful germs under your fingernails than on a toilet seat!

Someone's got long, mucky nails! They look like monster's claws — they'd better be cleaner than that to go to the party…

Wash, scrub, brush.

A kimodo dragon's claws are so dirty that just a scratch from them can give a nasty infection.

Someone's got very dirty ears!
And what's all this behind them?
Give them a gentle wash –
you can't go to the party like that!

Wash, scrub, brush.

Ears are very delicate and we have to be gentle when we clean them—just like rabbits...

Oxpeckers eat zebras' and other African animals' ear wax.

6

Someone's teeth are all sticky with food –
and smell that doggy breath!
Brush your teeth before we phone a vet!

Wash, scrub, brush!

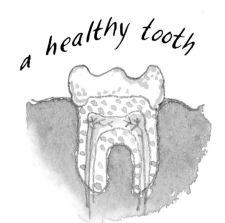

a healthy tooth

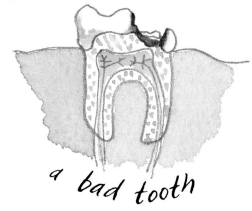

plaque builds up on your teeth. Add sugar and you make acid – that makes holes!

This grouper fish is letting small fishes clean his teeth – he gets clean teeth, they get a meal!

a bad tooth

Brush carefully twice a day and stop the rot.

Someone smells like they've laid a rotten egg – pooh! I'll change baby's nappy while you dash straight to the loo!

Wash, scrub, brush.

We need loo paper to wipe our bottoms.

Otters go to the toilet in special places to mark out their territory.

Someone hasn't washed their hands after going to the loo. You don't want to spread germs – or worms!

Wash, scrub, brush!

Kittens and puppies often have worms when they are born. They have to be wormed by a vet.

12

Tapeworms can grow up to 15 metres long and coil up inside your tummy.

tapeworm ⤴

Threadworms are tiny, and they make your bottom itchy.

threadworms ↑

Someone's been rushing around
getting all hot and sticky.
It's time for a refreshing shower…

Wash, scrub, brush.

Elephants have showers too – they
use their long trunks!

Someone else looks like they've been rolling in the mud! You can't go to a party like that! Shoes off. Clothes in the washing machine. Hop in the bath.

Wash, scrub, brush.

Hippos and many other animals use mud to stay cool or clean away insects!

Someone's hair looks like they've been dragged through a hedge backwards. It needs a good brush.

Wash, scrub, brush.

We can brush our hair to keep it tangle- and dust-free and looking good.

Even Arctic foxes like a good scratch!

Birds 'preen' their feathers every day to keep them in good condition, using a special oil from a gland under their tail.

Dandruff is caused by dry flaky skin and oily glands in your scalp.

Someone's hair looks a bit dirty.
Let's give it a frothy shampoo.
It will soon look clean and
fresh again…

Wash, scrub, brush.

A sloth's hair is a full of moss and lichen! It needs to be 'dirty.' This helps keep them hidden from danger.

Some birds like jays use ants to keep their feathers clean – ants squirt out a sort of acid that kills bugs.

Someone's got nits, poor thing.
It's not a big deal – nits love clean
people best of all. One last wash with
anti-nit shampoo will do the trick.

Wash, scrub, brush!

Monkeys groom each other's fur
and eat the nits – very tasty!

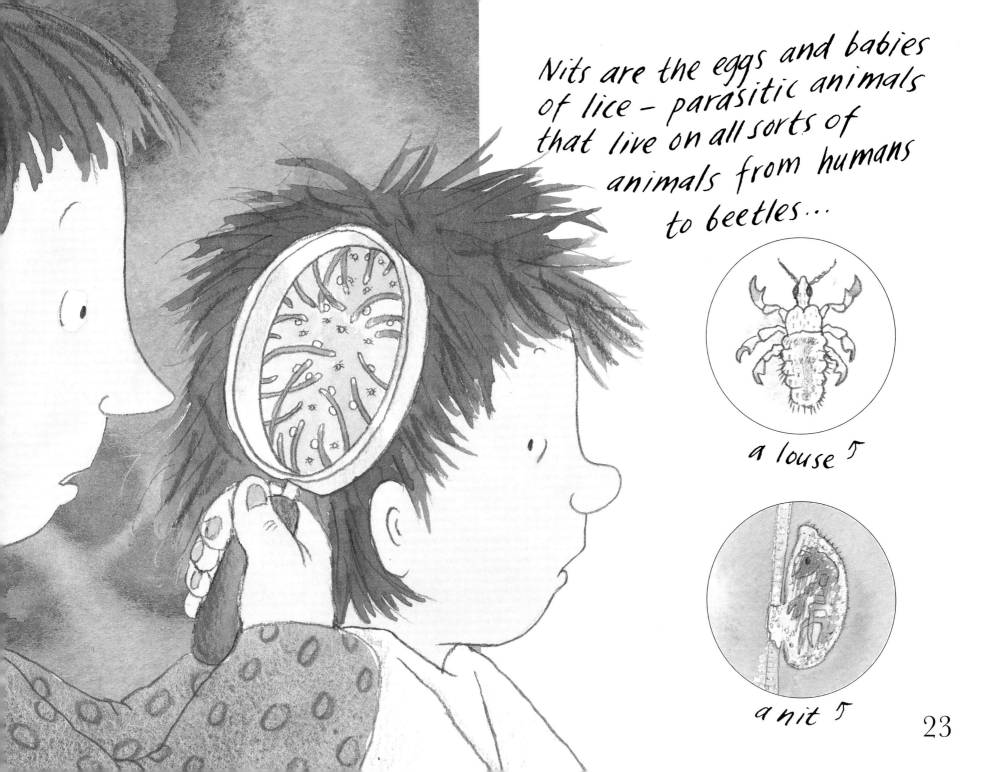

Nits are the eggs and babies of lice – parasitic animals that live on all sorts of animals from humans to beetles...

a louse ↰

a nit ↰

23

We all need to stay clean
and fresh. All it takes is a
little soap and water…
Every day!

Welcome to our Party!

Every day we need to…

Wash, scrub,
brush!

Keeping clean...

Feet
Clean feet and fresh socks - stop bacteria giving you smelly feet!

Clothes
Clean clothes - keep you fresh and feeling good!

28

Ears
Clean ears - help prevent earache...

Hair
Clean hair - keeps you looking and feeling good and prevents dandruff...

Teeth
Clean teeth - keep your teeth and gums healthy...

Hands and nails
Clean hands and fingernails - stop you swallowing germs and parasite eggs - or passing them to someone else.

29

Useful words

Ear wax is the yellow wax that builds up inside your ear holes. It protects your ears and helps you hear better. Other animals have ear wax, too (see pages 6, 7).

Germs are tiny plants and animals too small to see. They carry and spread diseases such as coughs and colds (see pages 4, 5, 12).

Glands are places in the bodies of humans and other animals which give out, or secrete, something such as sweat or oil (see pages 19, 20).

Infection is a sort of disease that is spread by germs (see page 5).

Parasitic animals are animals that live in or on another animal, feeding off it and laying their eggs on it. Lice are parasites, so are some kinds of worm (see pages 12, 13, 22, 23).

Plaque is a type of bacteria that grows on teeth and gums. When plaque mixes with sugar from food, it makes an acid which causes teeth to rot or decay (see pages 8, 9).

Tapeworms are a type of parasite. They are much larger than threadworms but not as common.
It is easy to get rid of worms with some medicine (see pages 12, 13).

Territory is the name given to the area a particular animal lives and hunts in. Some animals do not like to share their territory with other animals of the same type, so they mark their territory to tell others to keep off (see page 10).

Threadworms are white thread-like parasites. A person with worms gets an itchy bottom from the worms' eggs. If the eggs get onto their hands they can spread the worms to other people. It is easy to get rid of worms with some medicine (see pages 12, 13).

31

For Mia, Jan-Erik, Albin, Gabriel and André

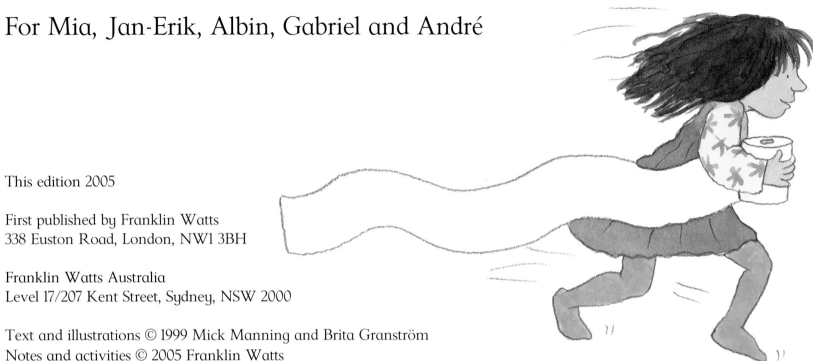

This edition 2005

First published by Franklin Watts
338 Euston Road, London, NW1 3BH

Franklin Watts Australia
Level 17/207 Kent Street, Sydney, NSW 2000

Text and illustrations © 1999 Mick Manning and Brita Granström
Notes and activities © 2005 Franklin Watts
Series editor: Rachel Cooke
Art director: Robert Walster
Consultant: Dr Michael Redfern

The illustrations in this book were made by Brita and Mick
Find out more about Mick and Brita on www.mickandbrita.com

Printed in Singapore
A CIP catalogue record is available from the British Library.
Dewey Classification 613
ISBN 978 0 7496 6225 7

Franklin Watts is a division of Hachette Children's Books,
an Hachette Livre UK company.